MW00463386

We hope you enjoy coloring this book.

Download some extra

free coloring patterns

and get news of upcoming books at

www.scribblepresscoloring.com/free-download

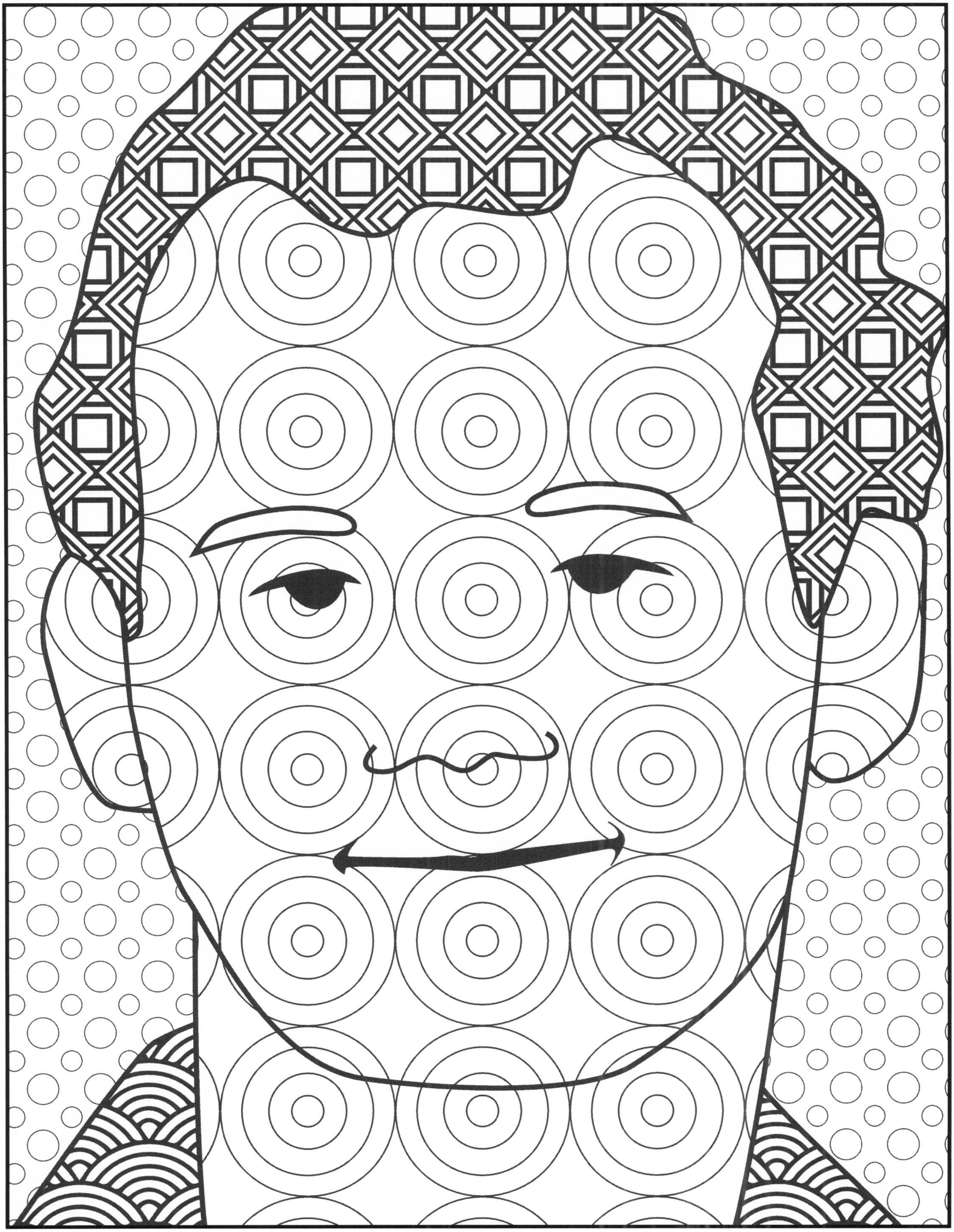

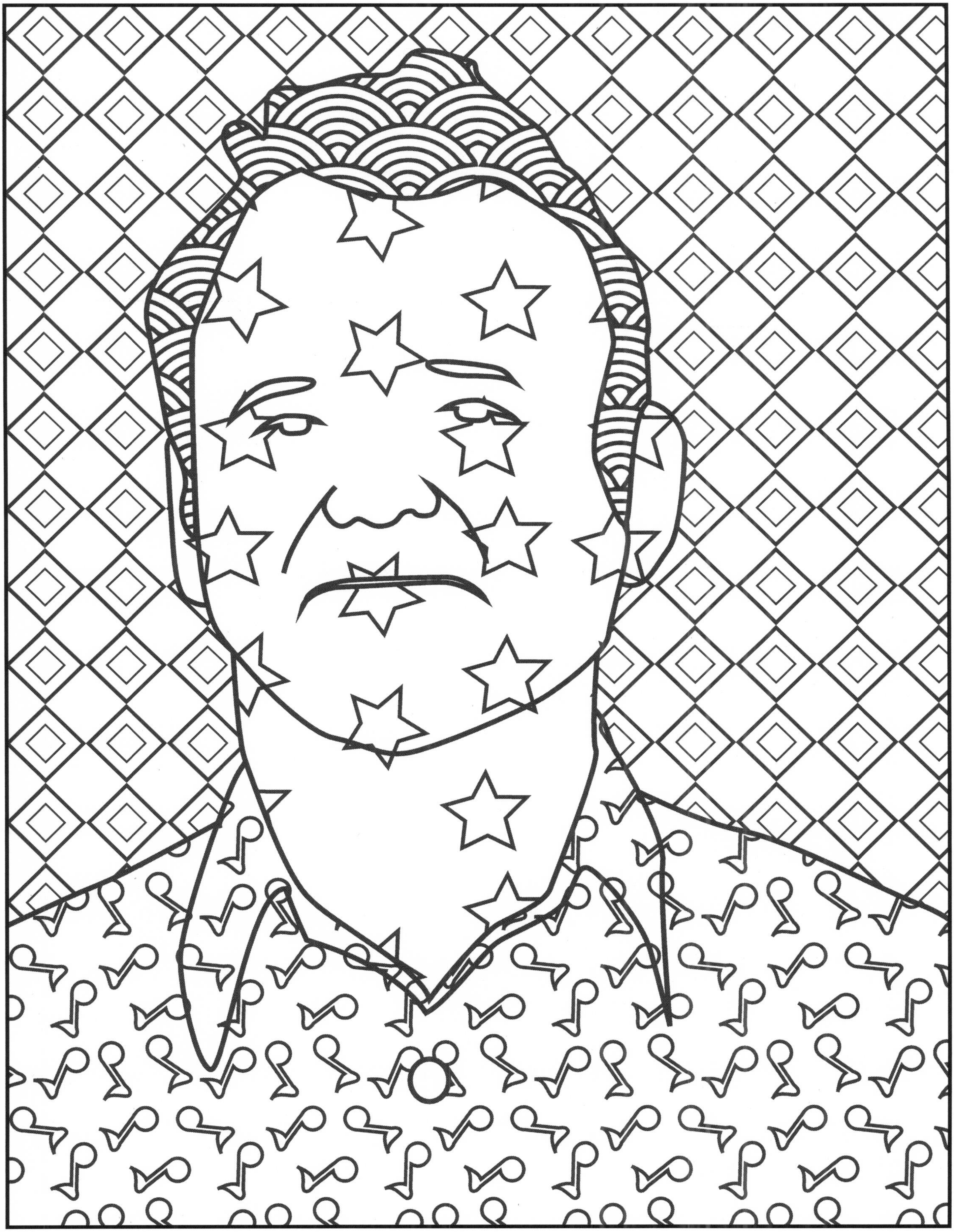

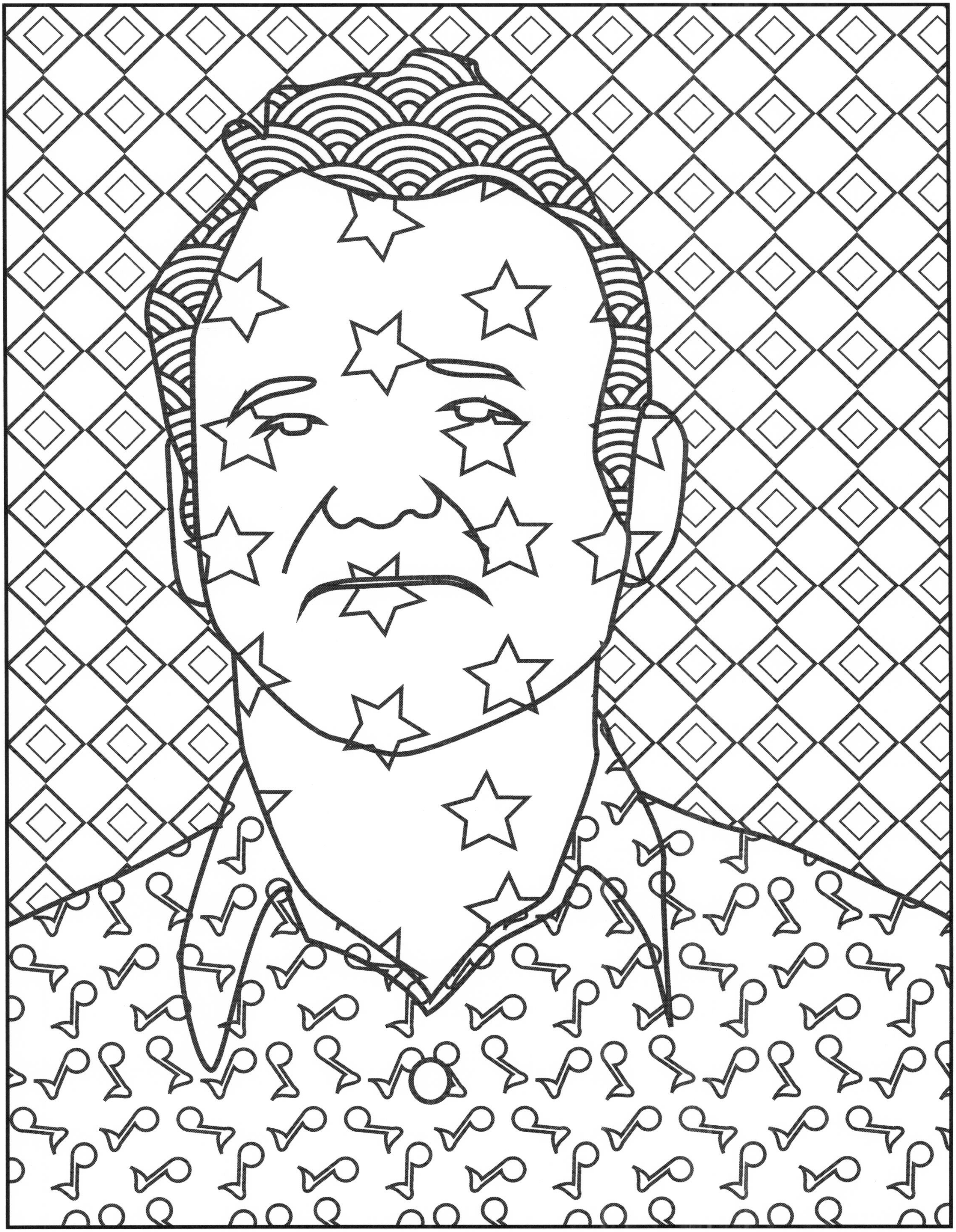

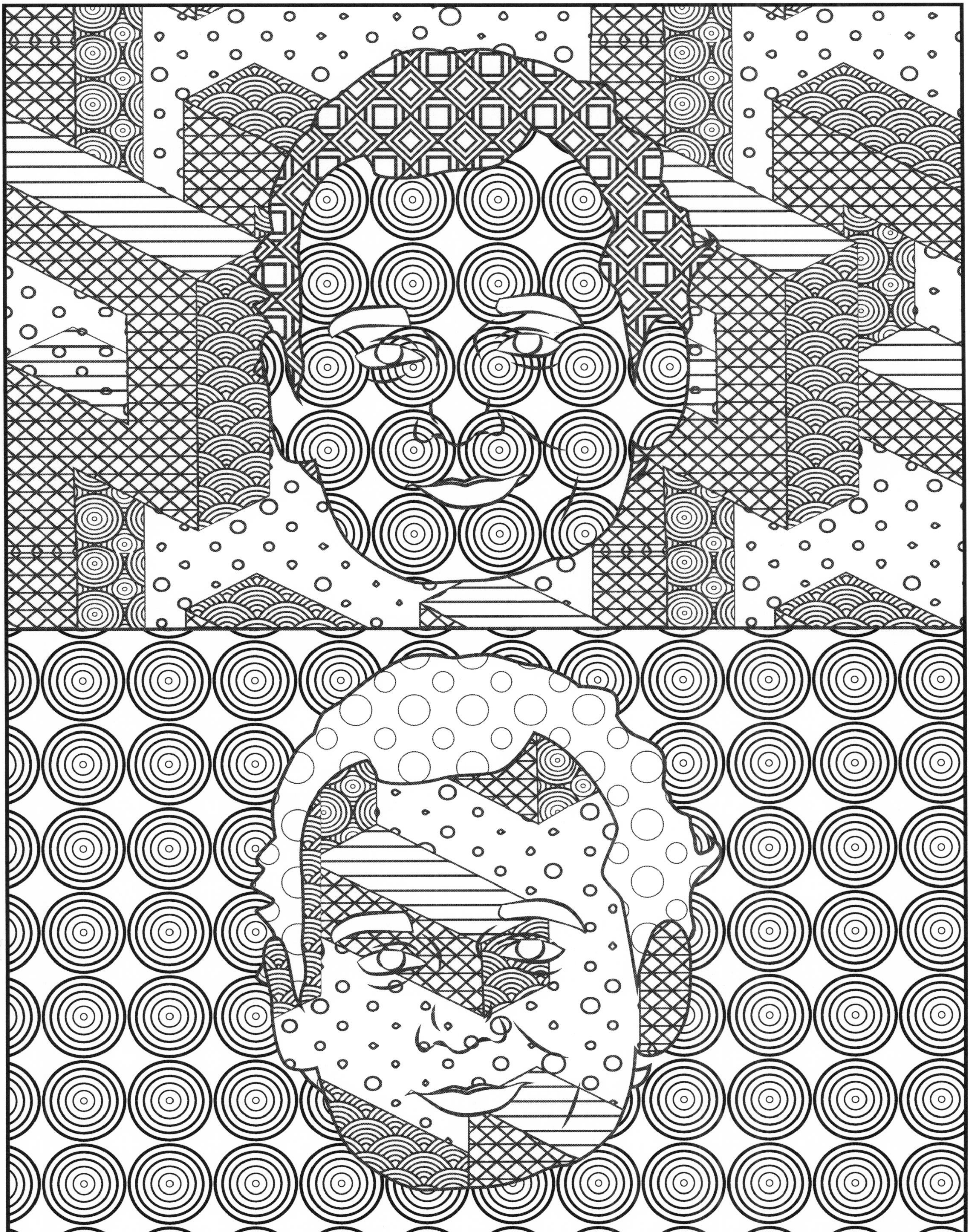

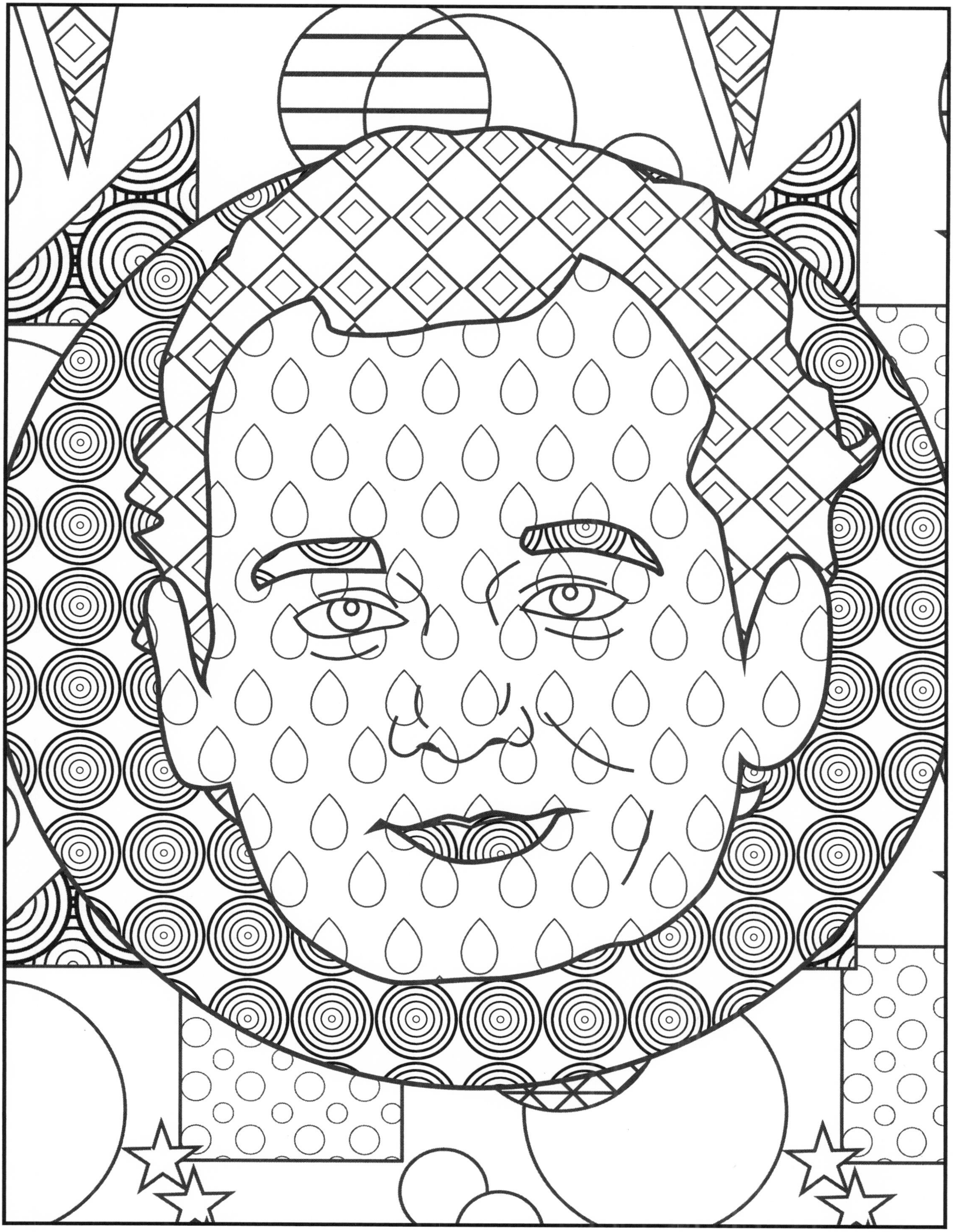

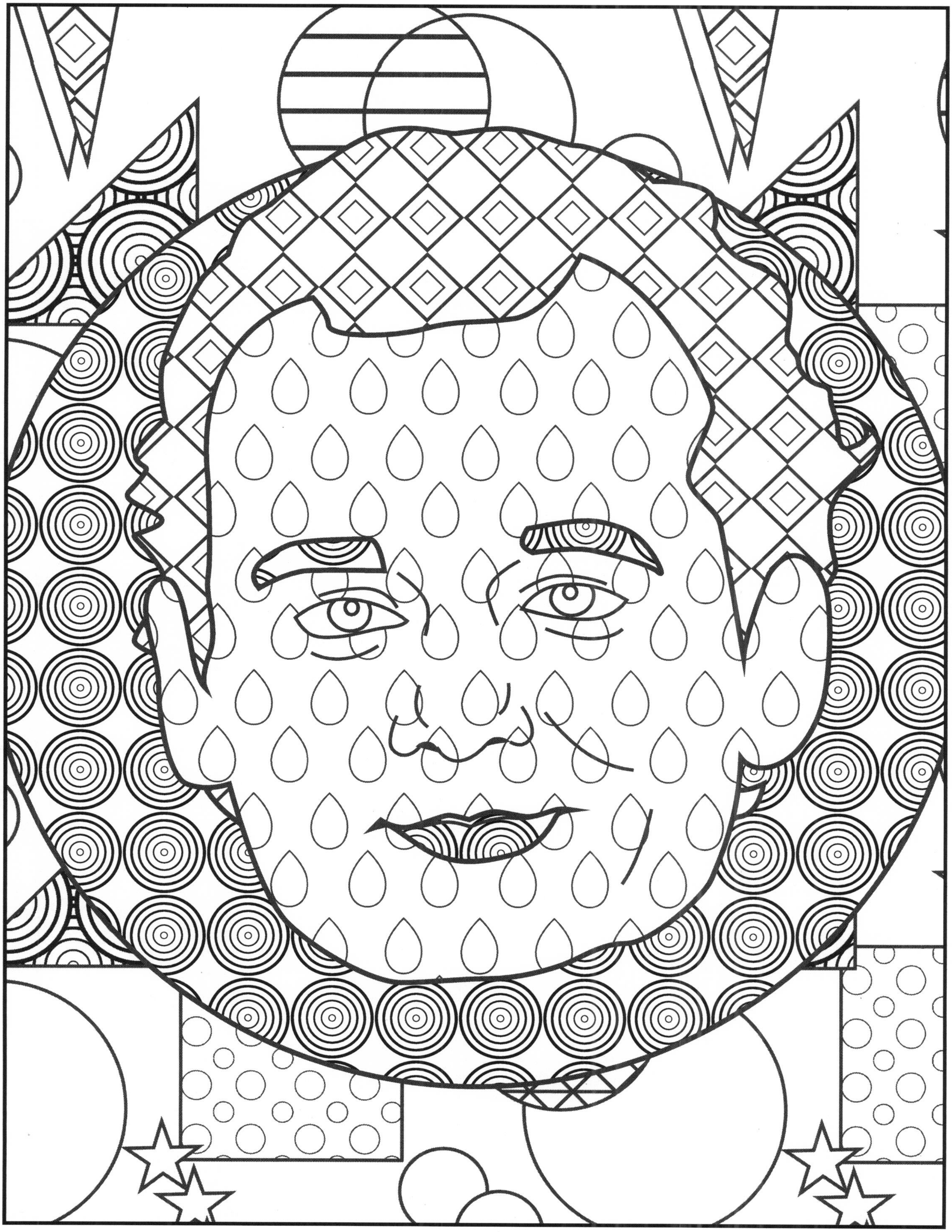

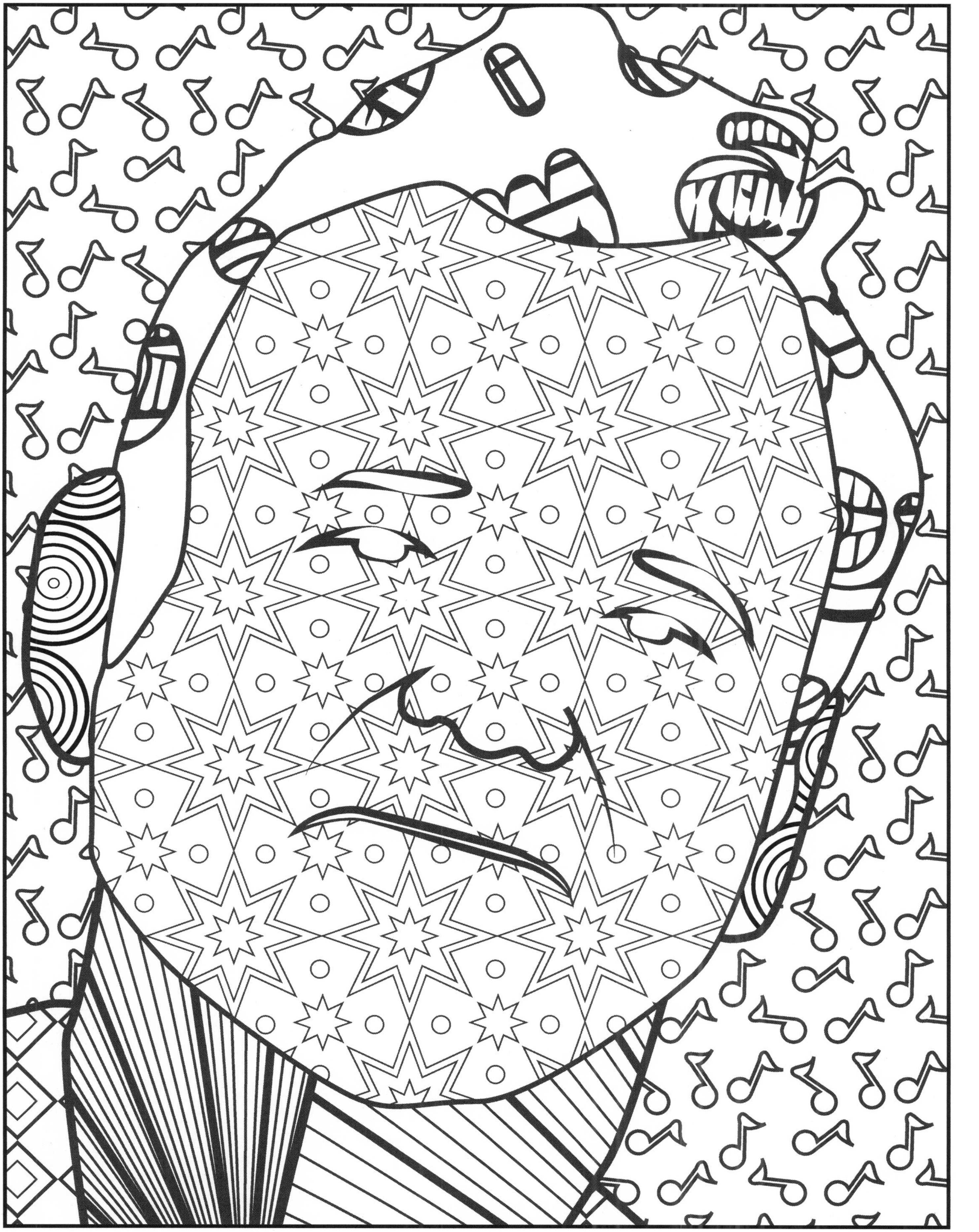

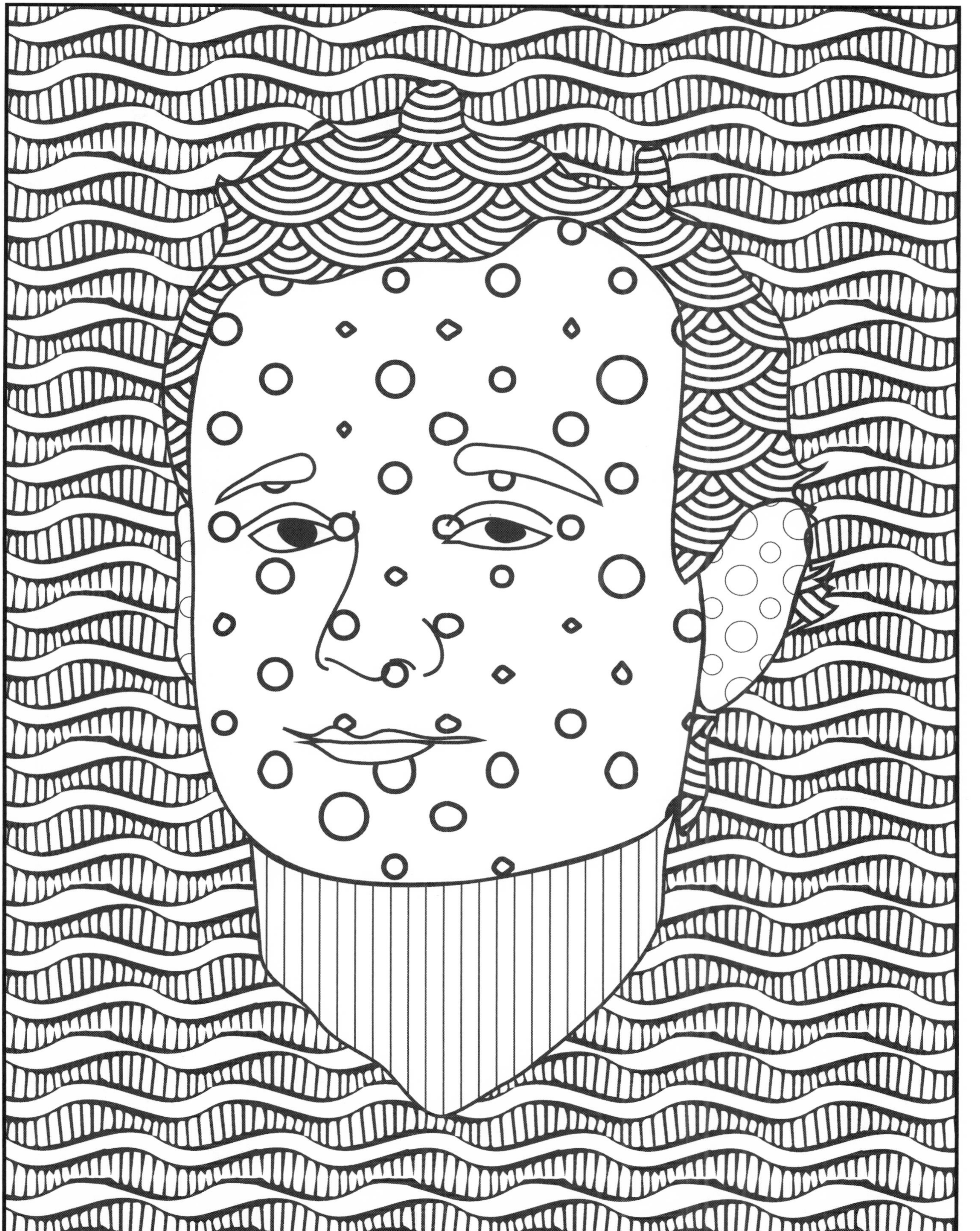

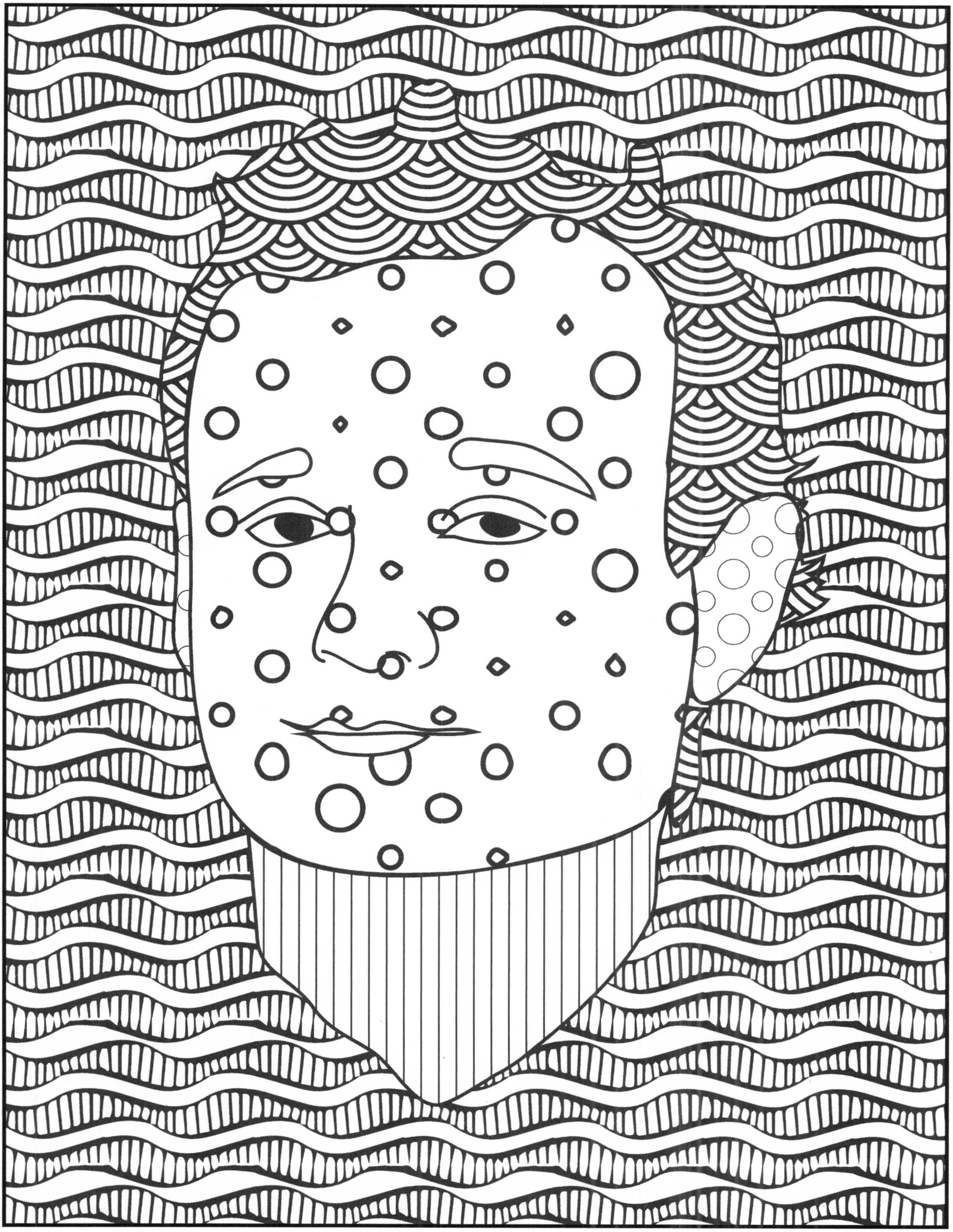

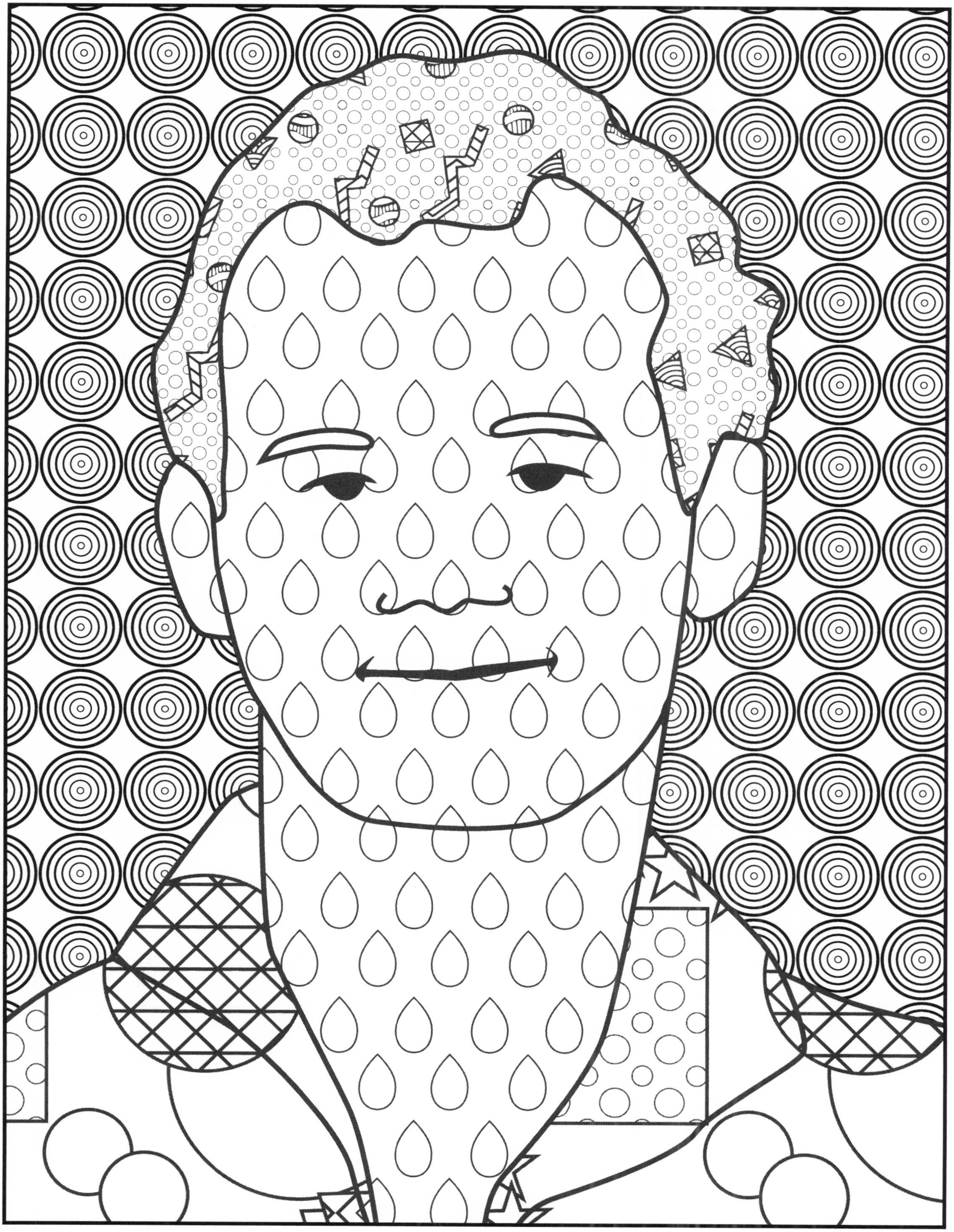

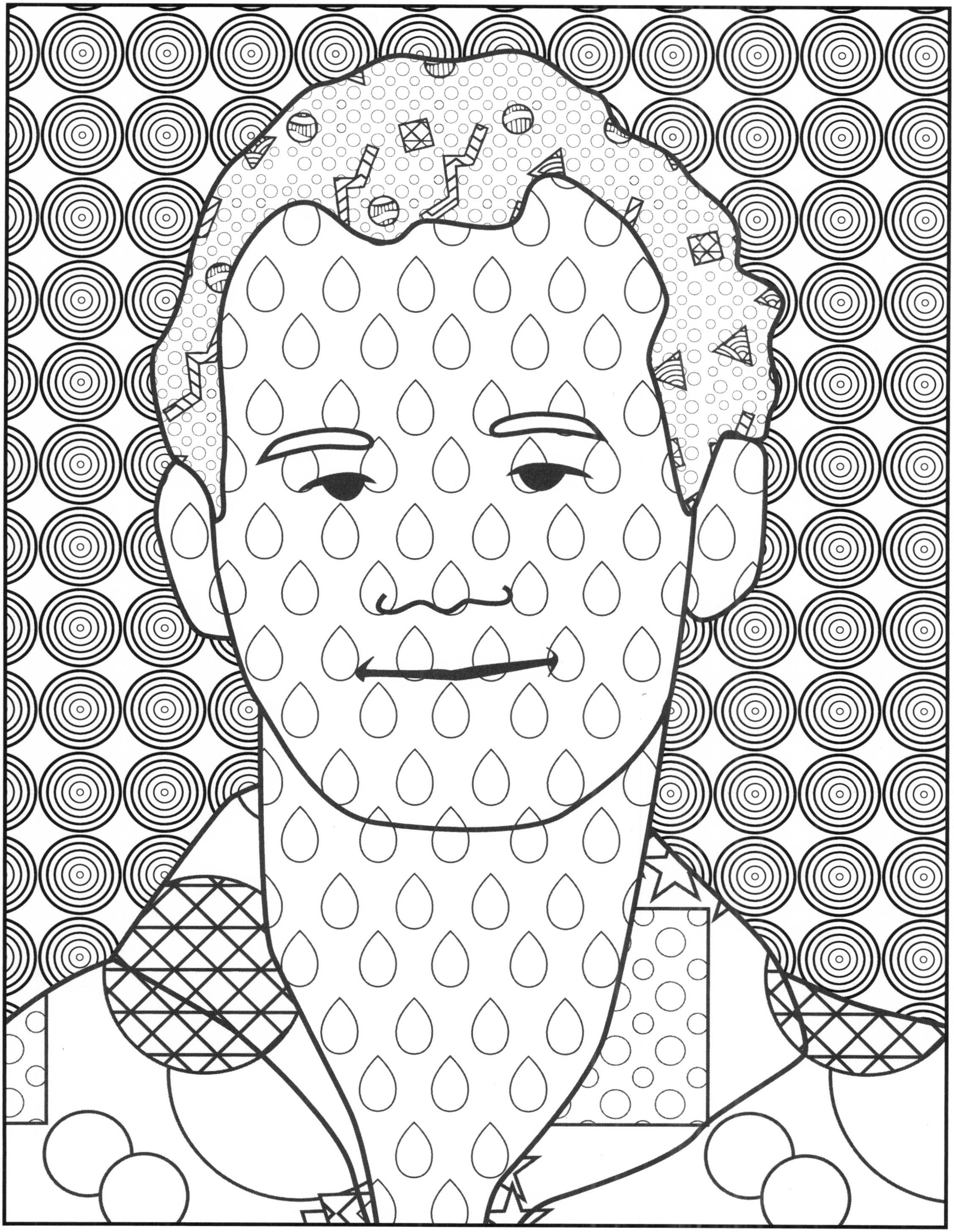

44612081R00038

Made in the USA
Middletown, DE
08 May 2019